the Word of Jesus

the Word
of
Jesus

DRAWN FROM THE DEEP WELLS OF THE SACRED TEXTS

MATTHEW, MARK, LUKE, JOHN

Closing Commentaries by
Douglas Koons and Gideon Devanesan

William Charles Publishing House
Saint Paul, Minnesota USA

The editors are deeply grateful to all translators of the New
Testament going back to those who first wrote about Jesus
from the oral tradition. We are indebted to the King James
Version of the Bible as a foundation in preparing the texts
for this volume. Changes to historic English verse reflect
contemporary spelling, language, and universal intent.

Calligraphy by Diane von Arx
Book design by Dorie McClelland

ISBN: 978-0-9844671-0-5

First Edition
01 02 03 04 05 16 15 14 13 12
Printed in Canada.

Library of Congress Control Number: 2010935523

PRESENTATION

the
Word
of
Jesus

In the beginning

was the Word,

and the Word was
with God. And the
Word was God.

He was in the

beginning with God.

Through him all
things were made,
and without him
nothing was made
that has been made.
In him was life,
and that life
was the light of all,

and the Light
shines in the darkness
and the darkness
has not overcome Him.

JOHN 1:1–5

I

AM

the bread of life.

All who come to me
will never go hungry,
and they
who believe in me
will never go thirsty.

JOHN 6:35

Come unto me
all of you
who are weary
and heavy laden,
and I will
give you rest.

Take my yoke
upon you,
and learn from me,
for I am gentle
and humble of heart,
and you shall find rest
for your souls.

For my yoke
is easy
and my burden
is light.

MATTHEW 11:28–30

You shall love the Lord
your God
with all your heart,
with all your soul
and with all your
mind.

This is the first and
great commandment.
And the second
is like it:
You shall love your neighbor
as yourself.

On these two
commandments hang
all the law
and the prophets.

MATTHEW 22:37–40

If you hold to my
teaching, you really
are my disciples.

You will then
know the truth,
and this truth
will set you free.

JOHN 8:31–32

Let the little children
come unto me,
forbid them not,
for the
kingdom of God
belongs to such as
these.

I tell you truth,
anyone who will not
receive the
kingdom of God
like a little child
shall not enter it.

And he took
the children up
into his arms,
put his hands on them
and blessed them.

Therefore I say unto you,
do not worry over your life,
what you will eat or drink,
nor about your body,
what you will wear.

Is not life
more than food
and the body more
than clothes?

Look at the birds of the air.
They do not sow nor reap
nor store away in barns,
and yet your Heavenly
Father feeds them. Are you
not more valuable
than they? Who of you
by worrying can add a single
hour to your life?

MATTHEW 6:25–27

To what shall we liken
the kingdom of God,
or what parable shall we
use to describe it?

It is like a grain of
mustard seed,
the smallest of seeds
you plant in the ground.

Yet, when planted, it
grows and becomes the
largest of all garden
plants having such big
branches that the birds
of the air perch in its
shade.

MARK 4:30–32

But I say unto you
who hear,
love your enemies,
do good to those
who despise you,
bless those
who curse you,
pray for those
who ill treat you.

To the one who strikes
you on the cheek,
offer the other also;
and from the one who
takes away your coat
do not stop them from
taking your tunic also.

Give to everyone who
asks of you; and
of the one who takes
away your goods,
do not seek them back.

Do
unto others
as you
would have them
do unto you.

LUKE 6:27–31

Who do the people
say I am?

—

Who do you say
I am?

Peace
be with you.

As the Father
has sent me,
even so I
am sending you.

JOHN 20:21

Rise!

Take up
thy bed,
and walk.

JOHN 5:8

Who is my mother, or my
brothers? Then he looked at
the circle of those seated
around him and said,

Here are my mother and my
brothers! Whoever does
God's will, the same are my
brother and sister
and mother.

MARK 3:33–35

Come,
follow me
and I will make you
to become
fishers of men.

MARK 1:17

All authority is given
unto me in heaven
and on earth.
Go, therefore and make
disciples of all nations,
baptizing them in the
name of the Father,
and of the Son,
and of the Holy Spirit,
teaching them
to observe everything
I have commanded
you. And lo, I am
with you always, even to
the very end of the age.

Enter through the
narrow gate.
For wide is the gate
and broad is the way
that leads
to destruction, and
many shall enter through it.

But
small is the gate
and
narrow is the way
that leads to life,
and only a few shall find it.

Why do you look at
the speck of sawdust
in your neighbor's eye
and pay no attention
to the beam
in your own eye?
How can you say
to your neighbor,
'Friend, let me
remove the speck
out of your eye,'
when you yourself fail
to see the beam
in your own eye?

You hypocrite,
first take the beam
out of your eye,
and then you will see
clearly to remove the
speck from your
neighbor's eye.

LUKE 6:41–42

Judge not,
and you shall not
be judged.

Condemn not,
and you shall not be
condemned.

Forgive, and you
shall be forgiven.

Give, and it will be
given unto you.
A good measure,
pressed down,
shaken together,
and running over,
will be poured
forth for you.

For with the
same measure you use,
it will be measured
to you.

LUKE 6:37–38

Lay not up treasures
for yourselves
upon earth,
where moth and rust
destroy,
and where thieves
break through and
steal.

But store up
for yourselves
treasures in heaven,
where moth and rust
do not destroy,
and where thieves do
not break in nor steal.
For where your
treasure is,
there shall your
heart be also.

Therefore . . .
be as wise as serpents
and as harmless
as doves.

MATTHEW 10:16

You
are the light
of the
world.
A city that is set on a
hill cannot be hidden.
Neither does one
light a lamp and put it
under a basket.
Instead, it is placed
on a stand,
and it gives light
to all in the house.
In the same way,
let your light shine
before others that they
may see your good
deeds and glorify your
Father in heaven.

MATTHEW 5:14–16

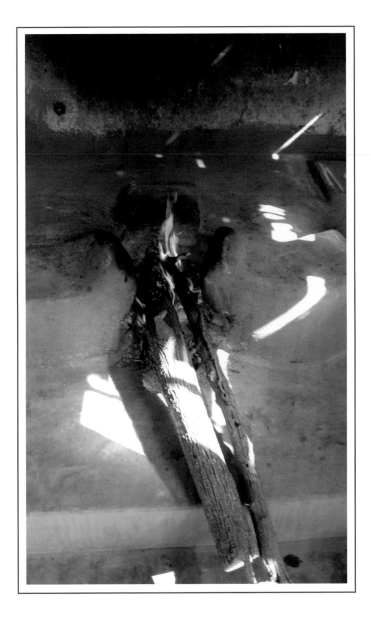

A certain man was going down
from Jerusalem to Jericho
when he fell into the hands of
thieves. They stripped him of
his clothes, wounded him,
and left leaving him half dead.
By chance, a priest was going
down the same road,
and when he saw the man,
he passed by on the other side.
Likewise, a Levite, when he
came to that place and saw him,
passed by on the other side.

But a Samaritan,
as he traveled, came where the
man was. When he saw him, he
took pity on him. He went to
him and bandaged his wounds,
pouring on oil and wine.
Then he set the man on his
own donkey; brought him to
an inn and watched over him.

The next day he took two
silver coins and gave them to
the innkeeper. 'Care for him,'
he said, 'and when I return,
I will reimburse you for any
extra expense you may have.

Which now of these three
do you think was a neighbor
to the man who fell
into the hands of thieves?
An expert in the law replied,
'The one who showed
mercy on him.'

Go and do likewise.

LUKE 10:30–37

Everyone who drinks
this water will thirst again,
but they who drink the
water I give them will
never thirst. Indeed, the
water I give will become
in them a spring of water
welling up to eternal life.

I am

the light of the world.

Whoever follows me
shall not walk in
darkness,
but shall have the
light of life.

If anyone
desires to be first,
the same shall be
the very last,
and the servant
of all.

MARK 9:35

As the Father has loved
me, so I have loved you.
Now abide in my love.
If you obey
my commands, you will
abide in my love,
just as I have obeyed
my Father's commands
and abide in his love.
I have told you this
so that my joy might remain in you,
and that your joy might be full.

My commandment is this . . .

Love one another
as I have loved you.
Greater love
has no one than this,
that you lay down
your life
for your friends.

JOHN 15:9–13

No one tears a patch from
a new garment and sews it
on one that is old.

If they do, the new
garment will have torn
and the patch from the
new will not match
that of the old.

And no one pours
new wine
into old wineskins.

If they do, the new wine
will burst the skins,
then the wine will run out,
and the wineskins will be
ruined.

No, new wine must be
poured into new wineskins
and no one after tasting
the old wine wants
the new, for it is said,
"The old is better."

They that are whole
have no need
of the physician,
but they who are sick do.

I did not come
to call the righteous,
but sinners.

Oh, you
of little faith,
why
did you doubt?

MATTHEW 14:31

Salt is good,
but if it loses its
saltiness, how can it
become salty again?

Have salt in yourselves,
and have peace
one with another.

MARK 9:50

No good tree bears bad fruit,
neither does a bad tree
bear good fruit.

Each tree is known by its own
fruit. People do not pick figs
from thorn bushes, or grapes off
brambles. The good person
brings good things out of the
good stored up in the heart. And
the evil person brings evil things
out of the evil stored up in the
heart, for out of the overflow of
the heart, the mouth speaks.

LUKE 6:43–45

No servant can serve
two masters. Either
you will hate the one
and love the other, or
you will be devoted to
the one and despise the
other. You cannot serve
both God and riches.

But when you give
to those in need
do not let your left hand know
what your right hand is doing,
so that your giving may be
done in secret.
Then your Father,
who sees what is done in secret,
will reward you openly.

MATTHEW 6:3–4

They who find
their life
will lose it,
and they who lose
their life for my sake,
will find it.

MATTHEW 10:39

And when you stand
praying, forgive
if you hold anything
against anyone, so that
your Father in heaven
may forgive you.

Blessed
are the poor
in spirit,
for theirs is the
kingdom of
heaven.

Blessed
are they who
mourn,
for they shall be
comforted.

Blessed
are the meek,
for they
shall inherit the
earth.

Blessed
are those who
hunger and thirst
for righteousness,
for they shall be
filled.

Blessed
are the merciful,
for they
shall be shown
mercy.

Blessed
are the pure in
heart,
for they shall see
God.

Blessed
are the
peacemakers,
for they
shall be called
children of God.

Blessed
are those who are
persecuted for the sake
of righteousness,
for theirs is the
kingdom of heaven.

MATTHEW 5:3–10

Behold!

A farmer went out to sow seed.
As he scattered the seed,
some fell along the path,
and birds came and ate it up.

Some fell on rocky land,
where it did not have much
soil. It sprang up quickly,
because the earth was shallow.

But when the sun came up,
the plants were scorched,
and they withered having
no root.

Other seed fell among thorns,
which grew up and choked the
plants so they yielded no grain.

Still, other seed fell on good soil. It came up, grew and produced grain, multiplying thirty, sixty, or even one hundred times.

They who have ears, let them hear . . . don't you understand this parable? How then will you understand any parable?

The farmer sows the word. Some people are like seed along the path where the word is sown.

As soon as they hear it, Satan comes and removes the word that was sown in them.

Others, like the seed on the rocky land, hear the word and at once receive it with gladness.

But since they have no root,
they last but a short time.
When trouble or persecution
comes because of the word,
they fall away in haste.

Still others, like the seed sown
among thorns, hear the word,
but cares of life,
the deceitfulness of wealth,
and desire for things
come in and choke the word,
making it unfruitful.

Others, like the seed sown on
good soil, hear the word,
receive it, and bring forth
a crop thirty—sixty—or even a
hundred times what was sown.

What do you think?
If a man has a hundred
sheep, and loses one of them,
will he not
leave the ninety-nine on the
hills and go to look for the
one that wandered off?

And if he finds it,
I say unto you,
he rejoices more over that
one sheep than the
ninety-nine that did not
wander off. Even so, it is not
the will of your Father in
heaven that any of these little
ones should be lost.

Or suppose a woman has
ten silver coins and loses
one. Does she not light a
candle, sweep the house
and search diligently until
she finds it? And when
she finds it, she calls her
friends and neighbors
together and says,

"Rejoice with me!
I have found the coin."
In the same way, I tell you
there is great joy
in the presence of the
angels of God over one
sinner who repents.

No one lights a lamp and
puts it in a secret place
where it is hidden,
or under a bowl.

Instead, it is put on its stand
so that those who come in
may see the light.
The light of the body
is the eye.

When your eyes are good,
your whole body is also
full of light.

But when they are bad,
your body also is full of
darkness. Take heed, then,
that the light within you is
not darkness. Therefore,
if your whole body is full of
light, having no part of it in
darkness, it will be fully lit,
as when the bright shining
of a lamp gives you light.

LUKE 11:33–36

Daughter!

Be of good
comfort.

Thy faith
hath made thee
whole.

Go in Peace.

He took a little child and they sat in the midst of them. Taking the young one in his arms he said to them, "Whoever shall receive one of these little children in my name receives me. And whoever receives me does not receive me, but the one who sent me.

I
am the vine.
You are the
branches.

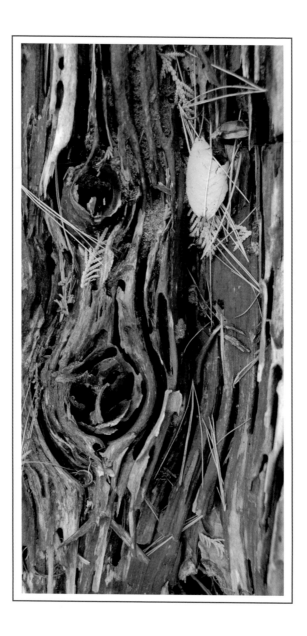

There was a man
who had two sons. The younger
of them said to his father,
"Father, give me my portion
of the estate. So he divided his
property between them. Not
much later, the younger son
gathered all he had, set off on a
journey to a distant country,
and there wasted his wealth in
wild living. After he had spent
everything, there was a severe
famine in that whole country,
and he began to be in want.

So he went and hired himself
out to a citizen of that country
who sent him to the fields to
feed the swine. He longed to
fill his stomach with the pods
that the swine were eating, but
no one gave him anything.

When he came to himself, he said, "How many of my father's hired men have bread enough to spare and here I am starving to death! I will arise and go back to my father and say to him: Father, I have sinned against heaven and against you. I am no longer worthy to be called your son; make me like one of your servants." So he arose and went to his father. But while he was still a great way off, his father saw him, and was filled with compassion for him. He ran to his son, embraced him and kissed him.

The son said to him,
"Father, I have sinned
against heaven and against you.
I am no longer worthy to be
called your son." But the
father said to his servants,
"Be quick! Bring forth the best
robe and put it on him. Put a
ring on his finger and sandals
on his feet. Bring the fattened
calf and slay it. Let us have a
feast and celebrate.
For this son of mine was dead
and is alive again.

He was lost and now is found. So they began to celebrate. Meanwhile, the older son was in the field. When he came close to the house, he heard the music and dancing. So he called one of the servants and asked him what this meant. "Your brother has come," he replied, and your father has killed the fattened calf because he has him back safe and sound."

The older brother became angry and would not go in. So his father went out and pleaded with him. But he answered his father, "See here, all these years I have been serving you and never disobeyed your orders. Still, you never gave to me even a young goat so I could celebrate with my friends. Yet when this son of yours who has squandered your property with prostitutes comes home, you kill the fattened calf for him!"

"My son," the father said,
"you are always with me
and all that I have is yours.
But we had to rejoice
and be glad, because
this brother of yours was dead
and is alive again.
He was lost but now is found."

Our Father
which art in heaven,
Hallowed be thy name.
Thy kingdom come.
Thy will be done
in earth
as it is in heaven.

Give us this day
our daily bread.
And forgive us
our debts, as we
forgive our debtors.
And lead us not
into temptation,
but deliver us from
evil.

For thine
is the kingdom,
and the power,
and the glory,
for ever.
Amen.

MATTHEW 6:9–13

Therefore whosoever
hears these words of mine
and puts them into
practice is like a wise
person who built a house
upon a rock. The rain
came down, floods rose,
and winds blew and
beat against that house.

Yet it did not fall because
it had a foundation on the
rock. But everyone who
hears these words of mine
and does not practice
them is like a
foolish person
who built a house on sand.

The rain came down,
floods rose, and the
winds blew and beat
against that house, and
great was its fall.

MATTHEW 7:24–27

I am
the good shepherd.
I know my sheep and
my sheep know me,
even as the Father
knows me
and I know the Father.
And I lay down my life
for the sheep.

I have other sheep that
are not of this fold.
I must also bring them.
They too shall hear
my voice,
and there will be
one flock
and one shepherd.

If you would
follow after me,
deny yourself
and take up your
cross daily and
follow me.

For they who would
save their lives will
lose them—and
those who lose their
lives for my sake—
they will find them.

For what profit
have you if you
gain the whole world
and lose or surrender
your very self.

Ask
and it will be given
unto you.

Seek
and you will find.

Knock
and the door
will be opened unto you.

For everyone who asks
receives.

They who seek
find.

And to everyone who
knocks
the door will be
opened.

MATTHEW 7:7–8

Fear not, little flock,
for it is your Father's
good pleasure
to give you the kingdom.

Sell what you have
and give to the poor.

Prepare purses for
yourselves that will not
wear out, a treasure in
heaven that will not fail,
where no thief comes
and no moth destroys.

For where your treasure is
there will be
your heart also.

Do not let your hearts
be troubled.

Trust in God.

Trust also in me.

In my Father's house are
many dwelling places.

If it were not so,
I would have told you . . .

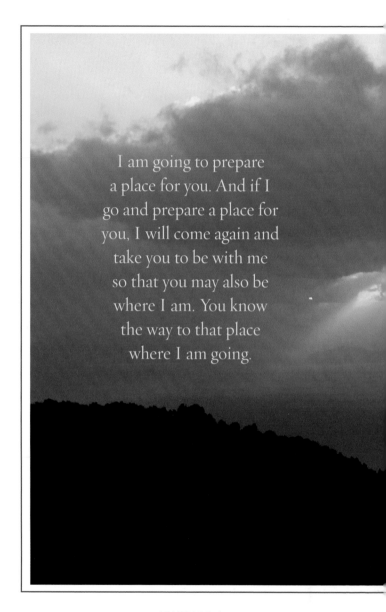

I am going to prepare
a place for you. And if I
go and prepare a place for
you, I will come again and
take you to be with me
so that you may also be
where I am. You know
the way to that place
where I am going.

JOHN 14:1–4

Jesus
often withdrew
to
wilderness places
and prayed.

Come with me
by yourselves
to a quiet place
and take your
rest.

MARK 6:31

And as they were eating,
Jesus took bread,
gave thanks and broke it
and gave it to the
disciples saying . . .

"Take and eat,
this is my body."

Then he took the cup,
gave thanks and offered
it to them saying,
"Drink from it all of you.
This is my blood of the
covenant, which is shed
for many for the
forgiveness of sins.
I tell you, I will not
drink from this fruit of
the vine from now on
until that day when I
drink it again with you
in my Father's kingdom."

MATTHEW 26:26–29

A new
commandment
I give you.

Love
one another.

Just as I have loved you,
shall you also love
one another.
By this all will know
that you are my disciples,
if you have love,
one for another.

Abba. Father,
all things are possible
for you.

Take away
this cup.

Yet not what I will,
but thy will be done.

Father,
forgive them,
for they
know not
what they do.

LUKE 23:34

It
is
finished.

Peace
I leave with you.

My peace
I give unto you.

Not as the world gives,
do I give unto you.

Let not your
heart be troubled,
neither let it be afraid.

Follow Me.

COMMENTARY
Douglas Koons

HOW SHALL WE TELL THE STORY OF JESUS?

This has been the challenge since people first met him as his public ministry began. Jesus leaves his home and walks. He walks in villages, on footpaths, the road, at the sea and on the riverbank, in the wilderness, and down the streets of Jerusalem. Virtually everyone he meets is a stranger. It appears that others are drawn to him as he speaks and teaches. Sometimes crowds form. Then there is also that solitary person he encounters whose life changes from that time on. Healing takes place. Some are saying he performs miracles. And so, the word of Jesus begins to spread.

One person tells another just a portion of a story about Jesus. Perhaps they were there to witness and hear him with their own eyes and ears. Or, a neighbor was there, and now it is someone else who retells what has been seen and heard. Always, the story is incomplete. Word of mouth is never finished. The oral tradition evolves into writing. A single written fragment, a handful of verses, chapters, a first book, then more, volumes upon volumes, the word of Jesus spills into time.

Today, the message of his life still needs storytellers who will carry on. In this present testimony to Jesus, it seems best to let him speak for himself. A limited gathering of verses, most of them where he is the speaker, form this volume. Teachings in parables, lessons, admonitions, commandments, and prayers are drawn together to give us a sense of his profound spiritual depth. The voice of Jesus comes through the message. We begin to hear it as we read and read again these verses from the Gospels.

From the many thoughts that are generated by this reading, three reflections are shared.

Humanity is much unchanged.

Jesus walked dusty roads and met strangers whose basic lives are much like our own. From the simple social exchanges between two people to the experience of loss among family and friends, we have most things in common with them. Yes, they talked about the weather, their aches and pains, and so do we. They grieved the death of that loved one, and so do we. Theirs was a time of wars and rumors of wars, and so is ours. While evil is universal and sin is personal, they tried to avoid the former and dismiss or ignore or repent the latter. Are we not the same? Celebrations of births and weddings and good harvests are quite timeless. In that age and our own, humans remain complicated. What appears on the top is not always what is going on at the bottom. We are a great irony like the sand held in the bells of an hourglass: generous and stingy, mean spirited and compassionate, thoughtful and mindless, destructive and healing. The word of Jesus is for our time and our humanity.

JESUS CALLS US INTO A LOVE THAT EMBRACES ALL. Love is the means of grace between us and with God. The admonitions not to judge others and to do unto our neighbors as we would want them to do unto ourselves are the blessings of a Divine experience. The religious tradition into which Jesus was born had a long history of covenants made and broken between God and the people. Pledges to do better and be better were all a part of those renewing relationships with the Divine. Observing the Law of God, as well as a personal aspiration to righteousness within the Law, became the essential norm. And yet, human frailty and failure resurface, and Divine judgment descends one more time. This cycle repeats itself until a new understanding ascends. Who better than God knows of the failure that is judgment? There is no future relationship if it depends on the ability of humankind to be good. For God, judgment of people and the nations no longer works. In and through Jesus, love does. And so we hear his voice speaking tenderly, "Love one another as I have loved you." This love of Jesus can be unsettling because it pulls down our defenses and invites us into a living, dynamic relationship that is enjoyed with God and shared with others.

FAITH IS A SURRENDERING OF OURSELVES UNTO GOD
AS GOD HAS SURRENDERED UNTO US IN JESUS CHRIST.
It is not about sets of belief systems created by various
Christian communities that must be seen as correct ways
to think of Jesus. For there is no idea or creed, doctrine or
theology that can adequately express the grace that is faith.
When we are scattered, disbelieving, and distracted by all of
life's intensity, God is present in our lives. As there is light
even in the shadows of the earth, God's grace is present
in our doubt. An early follower of Jesus was a man named
Paul. In one of his letters to the disciples at Corinth he
writes, "For now we see through a glass, darkly, but then face
to face. Now I know in part, but then shall I know even as
also I am known."

Just as the word of Jesus is an unfinished story, so is ours.
We still walk the paths of life, and many of us have been
on dusty, dusty roads. Our own lives are incomplete. They
are still in the making. With this in mind, *the Word of Jesus*
is offered as a means of reflection, meditation, inspiration,
and worship.

COMMENTARY
Gideon Devanesan

Though Jesus was a common person in appearance, he was extraordinary in real life. We have come to learn of him through his own words and from the witness of his disciples.

Some described him as teacher. Some thought he was a healer. Others identified him as a prophet. Still others were drawn to Jesus as comforter. The Gospels of Matthew, Mark, Luke and John all document varying understandings of who Jesus may have been. As there are now countless millions of people who have encountered him through his life story and the testimony of others, there are just as many personal understandings of him.

Layered into the Gospel of John we read passages where Jesus speaks the words, "I am . . ." The bread of life. The good shepherd. The gate for the sheep. The light of the world. The resurrection and the life. The way and the truth and the life. The true vine.

Jesus speaks with authority and boldness when he says the "I am." This witness to his identity then becomes a basic proclamation of the early Christian communion. "I am the true vine and you are the branches." These visually rich metaphors have since passed through the generations to the present age.

A closer look offers a deeper understanding within these texts of faith. For instance, Jesus as the bread of life feeds not only those who hunger and thirst for nourishment but also those who hunger and thirst for righteousness. He is with us in the choices we make daily. On some days, we may witness to others of our faith in him by standing against that which we know to be wrong. While most of us are cautious about such open and sometimes public dissent, throughout history there are women and men who have put themselves in harms way for the righteousness of God. Such believers in this Jesus have been prepared to face persecution and even death. And they have. A powerful understanding of these gentle words is not always easy for many of us to accept. Yet, the ones who do receive and practice faith in Jesus are promised an inheritance of eternal life, even if, at the extreme, they suffer hardship and loss because of their witness to that faith. The bread of life saves.

Being the good shepherd, Jesus is in action. He guides those who wander to green pastures where there is not only food and water, but also protection and comfort. This good shepherd knows the names of the sheep and the sheep also recognize the one who leads them. And when one is lost he seeks, and finds. Risking his life, he tends real needs with compassionate care.

My father used to narrate a story relating to a dispute between two shepherds. One day a few sheep were stolen from the flock of a poor peasant for whom the sheep were part of the family household as well as the source of livelihood. The sheep were found to be under the custody of another farmer who owned a large parcel of land and had cattle wealth of his own. Since both shepherds claimed ownership of the sheep, the case had to be decided by an impartial judge. The one who had stolen the sheep was sitting in one corner of the open ground. The other one who had lost them sat opposite. The lost sheep were tethered and kept at some distance. The judge remained busy investigating many other cases so the day wore on. By that time, the poor peasant who brought the case to the judge had fallen asleep.

When the name of the petitioner was called out several times, he woke up startled and started running up to the judge shouting, "I am coming, your Honor. I am coming!" At that moment the sheep heard their master's voice, broke the cords that bound them, and ran towards the poor peasant. The sheep found their true owner and stood with him close.

Now the judge did not have any difficulty in solving the case. Those sheep did not know anything about ownership claims or property rights. All they knew was the one who feeds them regularly and fulfills their essential needs of life, the one who nurtures and protects them. The case was settled.

When Jesus proclaims that he is the light of the world, he does so with radiance. The Light he gives is the enormous gift of life. Light does not show itself for its own sake but enlightens what surrounds it, transforms the darkness, and creates shades and color. It gives life and forms the fundamental source of energy that creates as the very light of the sun. This energy does not pollute nor exhaust itself. Even in situations of personal vulnerability and weakness we can feel it. In the light of Jesus we can experience exuberance of great joy with that energy. Light also symbolizes the power of Jesus as the Christ, who penetrates life and actualizes God's promise to be with us. His love is the eternal hope and confidence in humanity.

Once Jesus asked a profound question. "Who do you say that I am?" One of his followers known as Peter replied, "You are the Christ." The answer was equally as profound. As the Christ, Jesus is believed to be the savior of humanity and all of nature. For Jesus, this revelation came by the Spirit, the holy spirit of God. This message, that Jesus is the Christ, became the rock upon which he then built an early community of disciples, a community which later came to be known as the Church. With this one powerful question, and the short but clear answer Peter gave, it does not really matter what the rest of the world may think now.

Who you say Jesus is, and what you do in response, becomes that which really matters. Faith responds to a serious call given in a simple command when he spoke these words, "Follow me." It is a deeply personal call that has both social and universal implications.

One is moved to live like Jesus by helping others and serving the needy in compassionate solidarity and love. To follow Jesus also implies the surrendering of oneself to him, the Christ. In doing so, the believer is welcomed into the body of that community of disciples and joins others in a life of faith. We are not alone.

Each of the Gospels draws to its own close. Towards the end of John's testimony to the life of Jesus, we read the words, "It is finished." Though Jesus utters this from the cross, they are not words of defeat. While it is an expression of despair, it also assures that the mission is accomplished. The mission of accomplishment expressed by Jesus Christ refers to the condition of death on the cross in solidarity with the suffering of humanity. Where Jesus finishes, we move ahead in his mission.

Following Christ in this way, it is we who become the light of the world, a lamp that is kept on a hilltop for others to see. We become the first fruit of the new discipleship community that is continuously regenerating itself. Before us lies a very personal commitment and yet one that is fulfilled in fellowship with others. Together we mutually support the care of humanity and nature. As we do, God is served. This is the witness of believers as well as the reality of Christ abiding in and through us. A life of following Christ, then, becomes the embodiment of faith, hope, and love in action.

As Jesus said, "You are the light of the world." That burning of the light is an offering of the self. Having choices on how we live our lives, it is better to burn, and to burn brightly.

PHOTOGRAPHIC ARTISTRY

WE EXPRESS SINCERE GRATITUDE TO OUR LEAD PHOTOGRAPHER, JEANNE LEFEVERE, AND THOSE WHO HAVE FURTHER ENHANCED THE VISUAL WITNESS TO VERSES FROM SACRED SCRIPTURE: CAMERON QUINN, NATALIE GEHRINGER, AND DOUGLAS BAKER.

MATTHEW 11:28–30 ~ JEANNE LEFEVERE

MARK 10:14–16 ~ DOUGLAS BAKER

MATTHEW 6:25–27 ~ CAMERON QUINN

MARK 4:30–32 ~ JEANNE LEFEVERE

MARK 8:27 & 29 ~ JEANNE LEFEVERE

MATTHEW 28:18–20 ~ NATALIE GEHRINGER

MATTHEW 7:13–14 ~ DOUGLAS BAKER

LUKE 6:41–42 ~ JEANNE LEFEVERE

LUKE 6:37–38 ~ CAMERON QUINN

MATTHEW 5:14–16 ~ DOUGLAS BAKER

LUKE 10:30–37 ~ CAMERON QUINN

JOHN 4:13–14 ~ JEANNE LEFEVERE

JOHN 8:12 ~ JEANNE LEFEVERE

MARK 9:35 ~ CAMERON QUINN

LUKE 5:36–39 ~ JEANNE LEFEVERE

MARK 9:50 ~ CAMERON QUINN

MATTHEW 6:3–4 ~ JEANNE LEFEVERE

MATTHEW 5:3–10 ~ JEANNE LEFEVERE

MATTHEW 5:3–10 ~ JEANNE LEFEVERE

MARK 4:3–9, 13–20 ~ CAMERON QUINN

LUKE 8:48 ~ JEANNE LEFEVERE

LUKE 15:11–32 ~ JEANNE LEFEVERE

LUKE 15:11–32 ~ JEANNE LEFEVERE

MATTHEW 6:9–13 ~ NATALIE GEHRINGER

MATTHEW 7:24–27 ~ DOUGLAS BAKER

LUKE 9:23–25 ~ JEANNE LEFEVERE

MATTHEW 7:7–8 ~ NATALIE GEHRINGER

JOHN 14:1–4 ~ JEANNE LEFEVERE

MATTHEW 26:26–29 ~ CAMERON QUINN

JOHN 13:34–35 ~ JEANNE LEFEVERE

JOHN 14:27 ~ JEANNE LEFEVERE

DOUGLAS KOONS COMMENTARY ~ JEANNE LEFEVERE

GIDEON DEVANESAN COMMENTARY ~ JEANNE LEFEVERE

WE OFFER KIND WORDS OF APPRECIATION TO DIANE VON ARX
AND DORIE MCCLELLAND.

DIANE HAS CREATED A NEW WAY OF SEEING THE GREEK LETTERS
ALPHA AND OMEGA
AS WELL AS THE CROSS.

DORIE HAS PROVIDED HER GIFTS OF VISUAL PRESENTATION TO
PRODUCE THIS VERY SPECIAL VOLUME.

TO ALL THOSE WHO HAVE ASSISTED IN ADVISING, REVIEWING, AND
CRAFTING THIS WORK, HEARTFELT THANKS WE GIVE YOU NOW.